be inspired.
m
scrapbook colors
poppy

Published and Created By Making Memories
Executive Director: Paula Chen Su
Creative Director of Publications: Robin Johnson
Associate Creative Director: Gail Pierce-Watne
Art Director: Kevin Thompson
Associate Art Director: Anthony Hadden
Graphic Designer: Doug Seely
Writer: Jennifer Kofford
Copy Editor: Emily Waters
Photographers: Skylar Nielsen, Matt Reier
Step-by-Step Photography: Stacy Young
Desk Photo Stylist: Julie Reeves
Production Coordinator: Steve Billingsley

For information about bulk sales or promotional pricing, please contact Customer Service at 1.800.286.5263 or customerservice@makingmemories.com.

Printed in the USA.

ISBN 1-893352-10-2

FRESH PAINT

CreativeLibrary™

VOLUME 1

scrapbook colors

CONTENTS

Getting Started 8
Chapter 1 Edging 18
Chapter 2 Creating Backgrounds 24
Chapter 3 Altering Painted Pieces 30
Chapter 4 Foam Stamps 36
Chapter 5 Glazes & Washes 42
Chapter 6 Paint Surface Options 48
Chapter 7 Brush Techniques 54
Chapter 8 Stencils 60
Chapter 9 Embellishments 66
Chapter 10 Adding Texture to Paint 72
Idea Gallery 80
Artists and Author 94

"Paint has got to be the most versatile product I have ever scrapbooked with. If you want something to look new and fresh, paint it. If you want it to have an aged look, sand some paint off. Anything's possible with paint."

ROBIN JOHNSON

GETTING STARTED

the setup

Anyone can paint. And why wouldn't you want to? It's relaxing, creative and can even get a little messy. It's a hobby where anything goes and anything can be a masterpiece. Throughout the pages of this book, you'll discover simple techniques, out-of-the-box ideas and everyday inspiration for using this versatile medium. So find some space, gather your supplies and start adding a little fresh paint to your pages.

Inspire
to stir deeply; breathe life into
makingmemories
be inspired.

m
scrapbook colors
grapevine
manila
celery
shopping bag

1

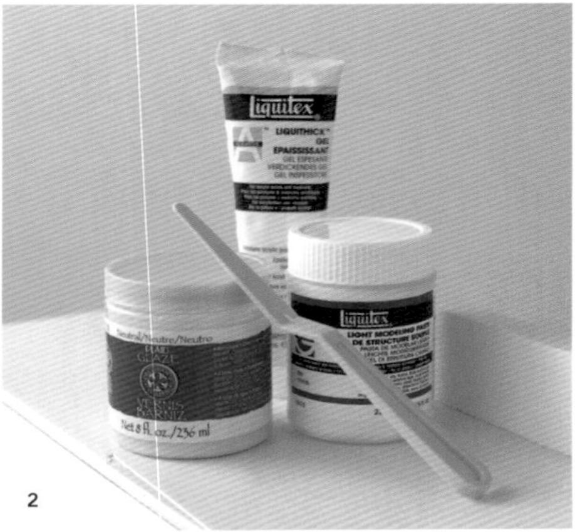
Liquitex
LIQUITHICK
GEL
EPAISSISSANT
Neutral/Neutre/Neutro
GLAZE
VERNIS
BARNIZ
Net 8 fl. oz./236 ml
Liquitex
LIGHT MODELING PASTE
DE STRUCTURE SOUPLE

2

A
B

3

4

1. PAINTS
Collect a variety of colors, always keeping primaries and neutrals on hand. They're perfect for mixing to create new hues or for lightening shades that are too dark or intense. Speaking of mixing, a palette is just the right tool for the job and keeps your colors organized and accessible.

2. ADD-INS
There are several types of thickeners, glazes and pastes that make paint thick or thin, shiny or sandy. Simply mix them with your chosen color of paint and layer them on for instant texture.

3. STENCILS
Whatever they're made of, you can use them with paint. Dab paint through paper, plastic or brass stencils or cut up stencils, paint them and use them as accents on your pages.

4. BRUSHES
Gather a variety of brushes—stipple, foam, flat, round, roller—in different sizes and shapes. They don't have to be expensive and you'll get a range of effects from each one.

1

1. ALTERING PAINT
Once you add a coat of paint to paper, metal or anything else, there's no rule that says it has to stay as-is. Change the look by sponging or combing while wet or roughening with a sanding block or steel wool when dry.

2. MASKING PRODUCTS
When masking, you want something that'll stick to your page, but won't tear it apart when you're finished. Choose low-tack or removable correction tape, found in office supply stores. Try graphic looks with hole reinforcements or other kinds of stickers or punch shapes out of paper, adhere with removable adhesive and paint away.

3. FOAM STAMPS
One of the easiest ways to start painting on your pages is to start with foam stamps. Simply apply paint with a foam brush, stamp image and clean with wipes. Choose from a wide assortment of alphabets and decorative sets to suit your layout.

4. BASICS
Don't even start unless you've got the basics handy. A water jar for rinsing brushes, wipes for cleaning off stamps or stencils and a plastic covering to protect your workspace.

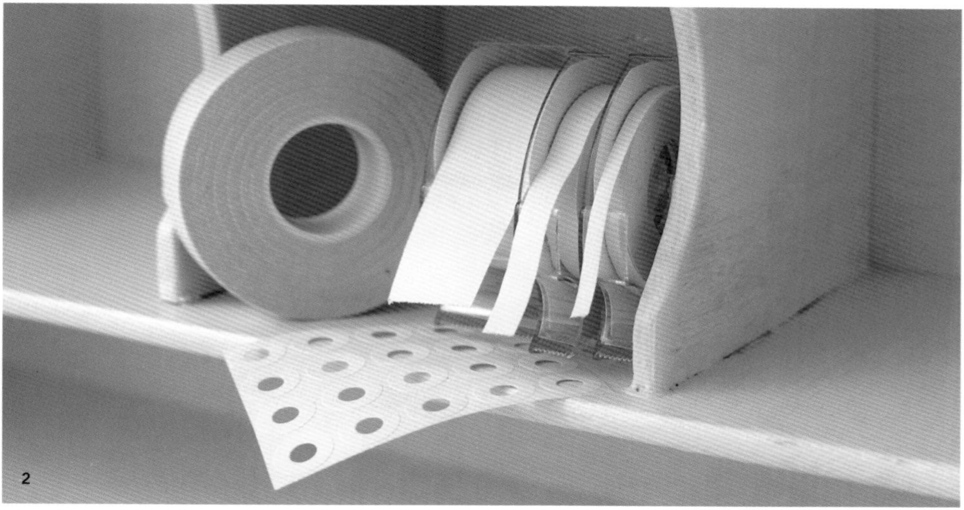
2

3

4

"I use sandpaper and acrylic paint in my house a lot. I just painted an old dining table and chairs white and it didn't look complete until I sanded some edges. My husband thought I was starting over!"

RHONDA SOLOMON

FRESH TECHNIQUES

1

edging

When it comes to acrylic paint, go ahead and be edgy. And we don't mean in the body piercing and midriff baring sort of way. We're talking about accenting outside and inside edges of shapes, letters, words and more. Edges are everywhere—you just have to look at things a little differently. With your octagon-shaped, yellow-tinted sunglasses, of course.

2. Using a foam brush, apply paint thickly to the edge of the photo.

3. Dab off excess paint onto scrap of paper. Edge photo further in with less paint on brush to achieve a spottier look.

EDGING IDEAS

1. Use tape to create crisp stripes on edges (see Backgrounds chapter for details).
2. Wash with color and edge with a thin line of paint.
3. Tear edge and paint to create a deckle effect.
4. Fold paper in sections, flatten and highlight creases with paint. Edge with a small brush.
5. Fold an edge, wash with color and paint the crease.

1. Select photos and mix paint colors as desired.

INTENSE JOY *by Erin Terrell*
Defined, foam stamps and scrapbook colors acrylic paint: Making Memories; Paper: Making Memories

how to: Cut random-sized circles and strips of paper. Dip a foam brush into paint and dab along edges. Adhere shapes to background paper. Edge photo with paint, mat and attach. Stamp title. Add paint to Defined sticker and attach.

1

2

3

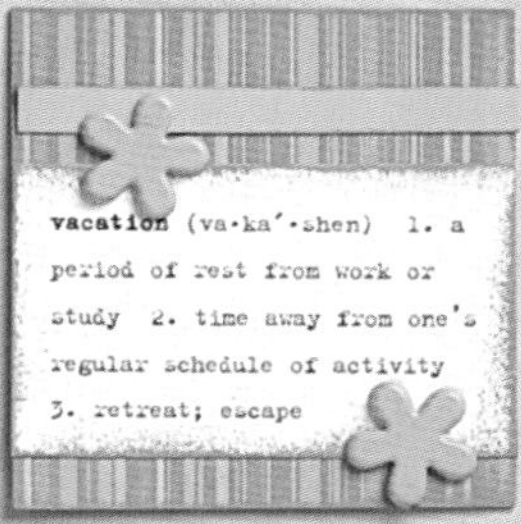

4

5

6

VARIATIONS *by Erin Terrell*

1. Stamp word with white paint and clean off stamps. Apply paint color to random edges of letters and re-stamp word.

2. Paint edges of canvas and wrap around background paper. Paint tips of Blossom petals and attach with brad.

3. Dab paint on outside perimeter of Defined sticker, adhere and add flower-shaped brads.

4. Edge bottom border strip with paint. Lightly sand and paint metal flower white, edge with color and attach with brad.

5. Paint metal edges of tag with foam brush. Dab tip of brush onto tag surface a couple of times to edge inside of tag.

6. Print journaling on transparency and using a foam brush, create a frame to highlight certain words. Apply paint to edges of transparency.

2

backgrounds

Do your backgrounds fade into the background? Pick up some cues—and some supplies—from the hardware store and they'll be interesting and eye-catching in no time. Mask off with tape, stickers or mesh to paint interesting patterns. Or use a foam roller brush to create a mottled, faux finish effect that'll take center stage.

DECORATIVE STRIPE PATTERN

1. With decorative scissors, cut a wide strip of tape in half. Place two pieces as far apart as desired width of stripe and paint background. Paint the stripe with a contrasting color.

2. Cut along one edge of tape with a second pair of decorative scissors, place along bottom and paint accent color on bottom edge.

3. Allow to dry and peel off tape. Decorate with metal shape attached with colored brad. Cut letters out to spell word and adhere.

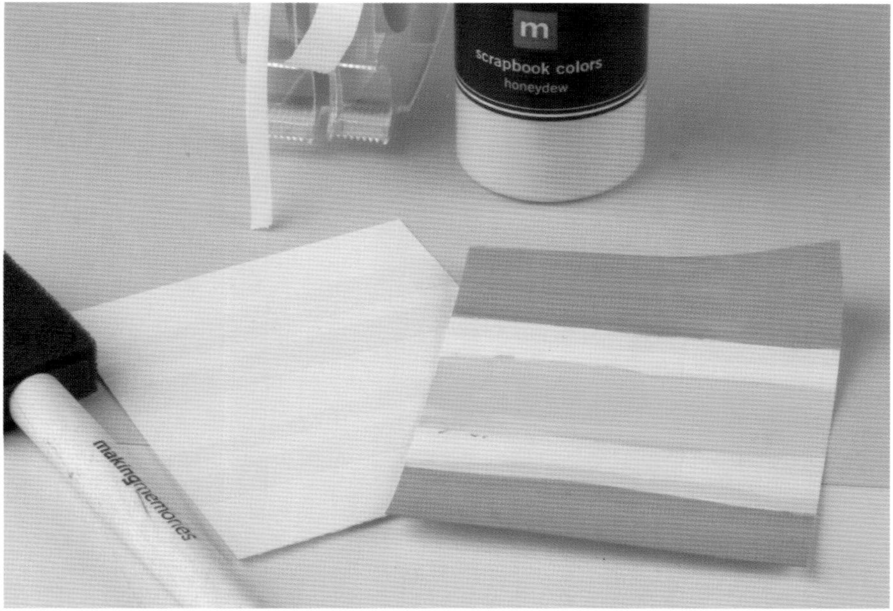

1. Using 3-M Post-it Tape, mask off various sizes and widths of stripes. Coat with paint using the widest brush possible in order to minimize brush marks.

2. Add contrasting color with smaller brush size. Remove tape carefully to avoid ripping paper.

THE GRADUATES *by Robin Johnson*

Alphabet stamp: Postmodern Design; Brad, moulding strip, ribbon corners and scrapbook colors acrylic paint: Making Memories; Corrugated cardboard: DMD Industries; Ribbon: Bucilla

how to: Create background using Straight Stripe and Decorative Stripe Pattern paint techniques. Paint Moulding Strips with white paint, allow to dry and rub to remove paint from circles. With foam brush, brush paint across surface of corrugated cardboard to create stripe effect. Mat photo and add ribbon corner. Edge second photo with paint, cut a slit in side, tie ribbon through and add brads to secure. Stamp initial on cardstock square edged with paint and tuck behind ribbon.

1

2

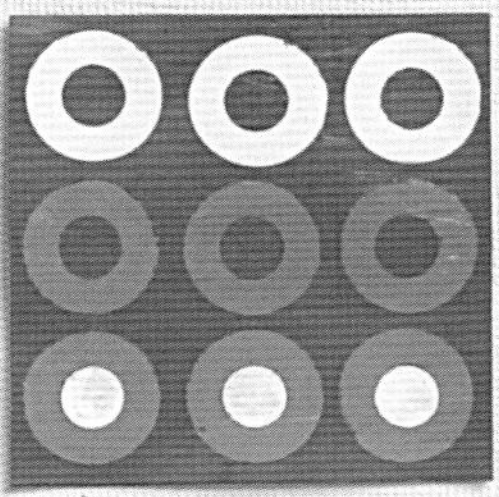

3

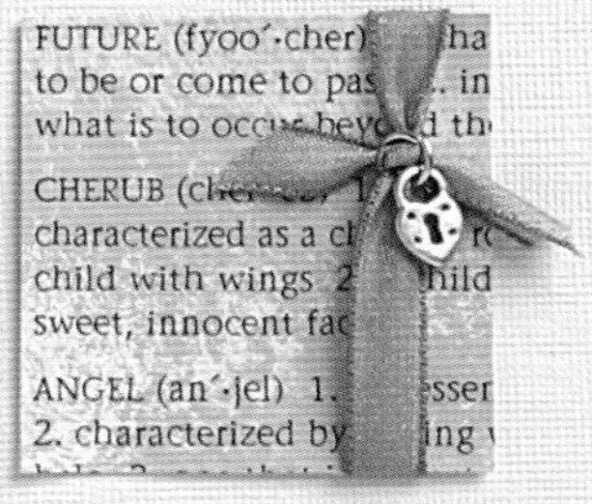

4

5

6

VARIATIONS *by Robin Johnson*

1. Create custom double-sided paper by painting white cardstock in two complementary colors. Rip edge and roll over to expose both colors.

2. Place a row of three paper hole reinforcers on white cardstock. Coat with medium pink paint. Add second and third rows. Paint piece dark pink. Paint centers of third row white. Let dry and remove stickers.

3. Paint Defined sticker with a small foam roller brush to create a mottled background.

4. Create gradation with a stippling brush. Dab contrasting color heavily on bottom and work upward, trailing pattern off gently.

5. Paint cardstock and cover with magic mesh. Coat entire piece in second color. Let dry and peel off mesh to expose pink pattern.

6. Gently paint across corrugated cardboard with a foam brush to create pinstripe pattern.

3

altering painted pieces

We change our minds, clothes and hair color. So altering pieces for our scrapbook pages makes perfect sense. Maybe the color of cardstock isn't quite right. Or the clean look of polished metal doesn't quite fit with the shabby style you're going for. There's no rule that says everything must be used as-is. With a little paint and a touch of imagination, you can give any piece an extreme makeover.

HEAT EMBOSSING

1. Sand metal with sanding block. Paint metal with first coat of paint. Let dry and add second coat.

2. Using Versamark ink, stamp image onto metal.

3. Coat with bronze Ultra Thick Embossing Enamel and heat set.

1. Paint a thick layer of paint for base color. This will be what shows through the crackling. Let dry completely.

2. Apply crackle medium and let dry according to package directions (times vary with each manufacturer). Piece will still be tacky. Do not let it dry thoroughly.

3. Paint on top coat of contrasting color. Brush it on carefully, using a minimal amount of strokes. Going over and over the piece will "smear" the crackle. Once applied, crackling will slowly appear. This technique works on a variety of surfaces including paper and metal.

IMAGINE, HOPE *by Rhonda Solomon*

Cardstock tags, metal words and scrapbook colors acrylic paint: Making Memories; Paper: Bazzill and K&Company; Other: Embroidery floss, flowers, ribbon and silver beads

how to: Cut frame out of cardstock. Paint frame and Metal Words using Crackling technique. Adhere words to bottom corner of frame. In opposite corner, wrap floss and ribbon around frame, add mini painted and printed tags and tie or knot. Attach flowers to corners using silver beads as centers. Place frame on background paper and center photo inside.

1 2 3

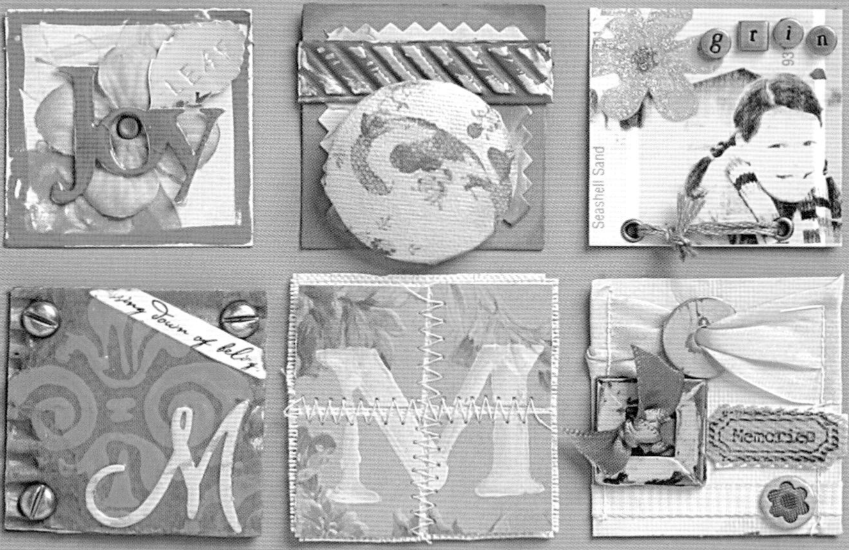

4 5 6

VARIATIONS *by Rhonda Solomon*

1. Paint Metal Word and emboss with Ultra Thick Embossing Enamel. Paint on Metal Sheet, punch out leaf shape and stamp word in metal.

2. Stamp fabric with foam stamp and create button using a button kit. Paint Moulding Strip and sand to remove paint from raised areas.

3. Stamp flower with paint, add embossing powder and let sit. Not heating gives image a sandy texture.

4. Paint Eyelet Letter and sand. Place on cardboard that's been stamped with image and cover with decoupage medium.

5. Stamp letter on patterned paper and cut into four equal pieces. Zigzag stitch back together.

6. Coat metal embellishments with multiple layers of paint. When dry, lightly sand.

4

foam stamps

If you're not a stamper, foam stamps will convert you. Coat the entire surface or paint just a portion to create softened backgrounds, borders, accents and more. And with such a wide range of choices on the market—everything from decorative stamps to alphabet sets—there's no end to what you can create. Once you get going, you won't want to stop.

JUST ME & DAD *by Robin Johnson*

Alphabet rub-ons, decorative brad, eyelets, foam stamps, magnetic ornament stamp, ribbon and scrapbook colors acrylic paint: Making Memories

how to: Tear paper and adhere pieces to background. Edge perimeter with paint. Paint three squares and place photo on top. Use eyelets and ribbon to decorate top corner. Stamp flower using Outlining Stamps technique. Stamp title using Color Gradation technique. Complete title with alphabet rub-ons and ornament stamp. Cut out tag shape, stamp flower on corner and edge with white paint. Add journaling and finish with Decorative Brad and ribbon.

1. Paint letters two-thirds of the way down with light paint color.

2. Paint a complementary color two-thirds of the way up the letters.

3. Where colors overlap, paints will blend, creating a third hue.

OUTLINING STAMPS

1. Paint stamp with base color using foam brush.

2. Before paint dries, paint outline of stamp using a small brush and contrasting paint color.

3. Press stamp evenly and quickly onto desired surface.

1

2

3

4

5

6

VARIATIONS *by Robin Johnson*

1. Paint only a portion of stamp when small image is needed. Try using multiple colors on one stamp.

2. After stamping an image with paint, stamp it again with watermark ink. Add embossing powder and heat set.

3. Use foam stamps on all types of fabric as well as on paper.

4. Create a shadow effect behind letters by stamping in a lighter color first. Then offset and stamp in a darker color.

5. Dry brush color onto stamp for a more aged look.

6. After stamping a letter, create a template to add pattern inside. Stamp image onto scrap cardstock, cut out with craft knife and place over original letter. Use stencil to add stripes, polka dots, etc.

5

glazes & washes

Visit any home improvement store or flip through the latest decorating magazines and it's plain to see that faux finishing using glazes and washes is all the rage. They're easy to use, never have to be perfect and mask a multitude of sins. They add depth, character and texture to whatever they touch. If you love what they do for your décor, just imagine what they'll do for your scrapbook.

FAUX LEATHER

1. Cut piece of mulberry paper slightly larger than background. Crinkle mulberry paper several times. Mix paint and glaze together at a 1:1 ratio.

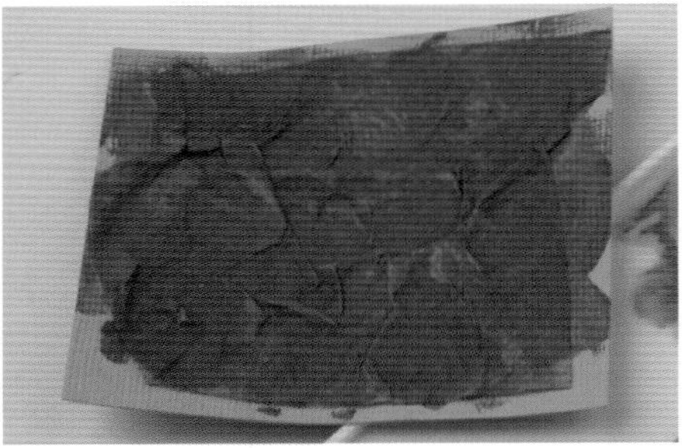

2. Lay mulberry paper on cardstock and paint on glaze, making sure paper is forming large creases. It should not be painted down flat.

3. Immediately remove mulberry paper and leather-like pattern will be left behind. Repeat on other areas with same piece of paper to cover background if necessary.

1. Cover entire paper with light coat of water. For best results, use watercolor paper.

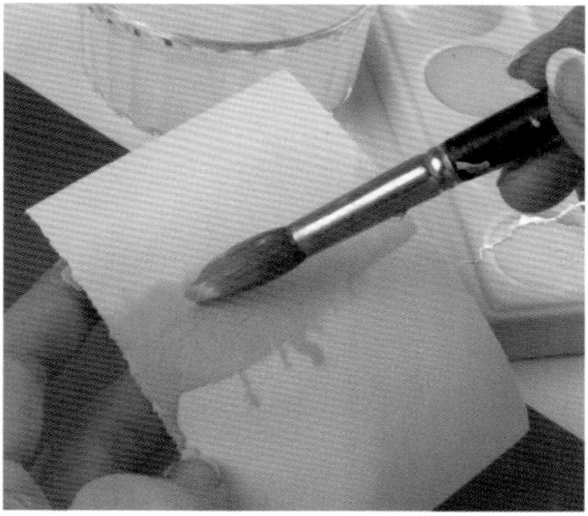

2. Thin desired paint colors with small amount of water. Start painting with lightest color and gradually blend into medium tone.

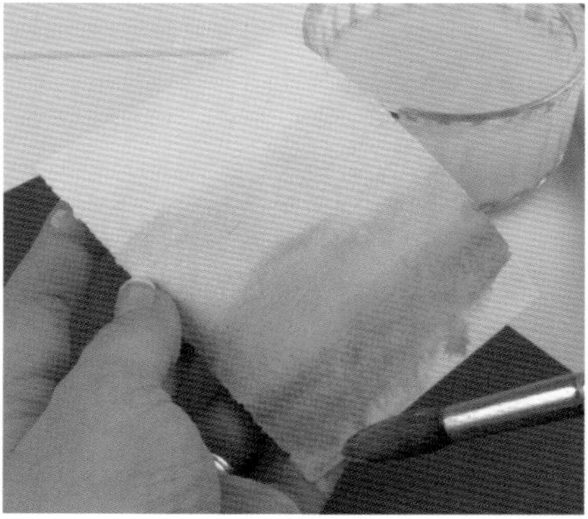

3. Continue painting, working quickly, so water does not dry. Paint from medium tone to darkest color to complete the wash.

4. Allow to dry. Vary the amounts of water and paint for different effects.

GOTCHA *by Rhonda Solomon*

Magnetic date stamp, scrapbook colors acrylic paint and stamping ink: Making Memories; Photo corners: Canson; Stamps: All Night Media; Other: Rope

how to: Use the Faux Leather technique to create background texture and let dry. Double mat large sepia toned photograph, rub black ink along edges of both mats and stamp date. Add photo corners. Stamp title with acrylic paint, using squares of cardstock for some of the letters. Punch holes in top corners of mat and background paper and tie rope through with knots to attach.

1

2

3

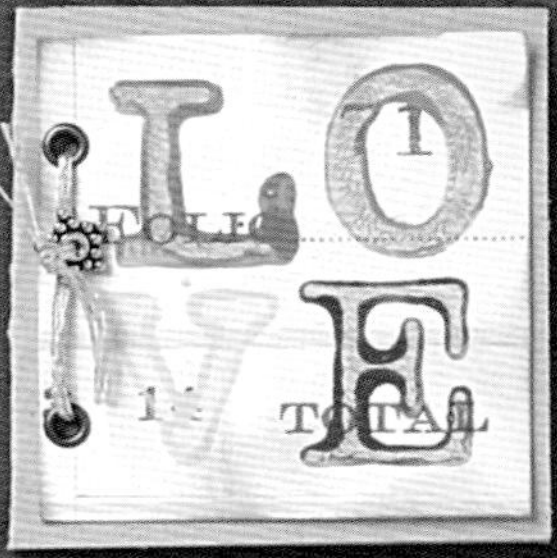

4

5

6

VARIATIONS *by Rhonda Solomon*

1. Stamp words with art masking fluid. Wash over surface with diluted paint and let dry. Erase over to pick up masking fluid, leaving resisted image.

2. Add glaze to paint and color raised surfaces and background of molded paper art.

3. Mix paint with glaze and use to stamp letters and edge paper.

4. Dilute several colors of acrylic paint with water and wash across old book paper.

5. Crinkle and flatten printed tissue paper and coat heavily with paint mixed with glaze. Let dry, sand slightly and add one layer of decoupage matte medium to create interesting background.

6. Stamp background image with stamp and heat emboss. Mix glaze and paint and brush over top.

6

paint surface options

The world is your canvas and you're the artist. Just about any surface can be coated with paint—the key is experimentation. Brush it on paper, smear it on metal, dab it on fabric and smudge it everywhere in between. Let go of inhibitions, abandon the rules and start creating your own unique works of art.

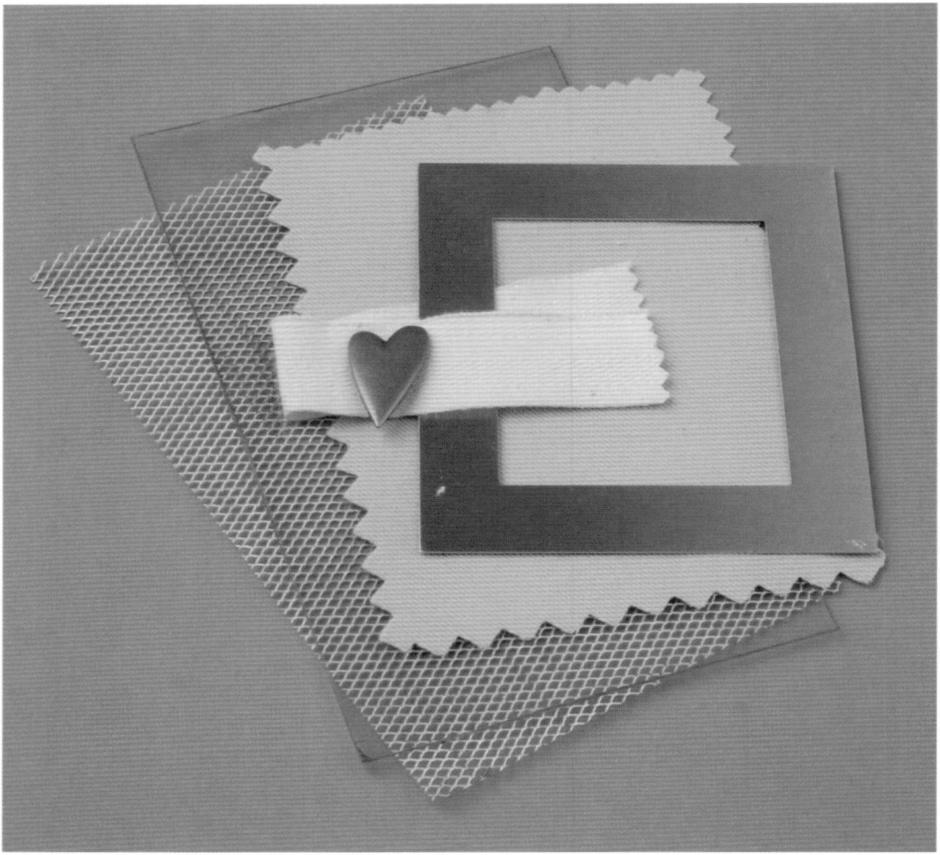

5. Besides paper, try painting on a variety of surfaces such as wire mesh, transparencies, canvas, metals, fabric and twill tape.

1. Apply one coat of acrylic paint to watercolor paper with foam brush and let dry.

2. Paint on a second coat and let dry. Cut paper into strips and adhere to background cardstock. Dry brush more paint over entire surface with stiff paintbrush.

3. Paint Metal Mesh and let dry.

4. Attach mesh to page with Metal Glue.

SUMMER 2003—HAVING FUN *by Erin Terrell*

Alphabet stamps: PSX Design; Artisan label, blossom, brad, cardstock tags, eyelet, jump ring, magnetic date stamp, metal mesh, ribbon, safety pin, scrapbook colors acrylic paint, staples and washer word: Making Memories; Paper: Bazzill; Stamping ink: Ranger Industries; Tags: Rusty Pickle; Watercolor paper: Strathmore

how to: Wipe acrylic paint along edges of background paper. Paint paper using Painting on Watercolor Paper technique, trim into long, thin strips and adhere to background. Dry brush paint over entire surface. Paint Metal Mesh, fold a section of cardstock along top and staple to secure. Cut photo mat and paint. Edge photo with same color and mount. Tie ribbon through aged tags and wrap around side. Rub paint into Washer Word and hang from ribbon with jump ring. Paint edges of Artisan Label, stamp title, date and attach. Join tags with eyelet and hang from mesh with safety pin, ribbon and jump ring. Attach flower with brad.

1 

4 

2 

5 

3 

6 

VARIATIONS *by Erin Terrell*

1. Dry brush background paper. Paint watercolor paper and place along bottom. Edge photo and section of Defined sticker with same color. Rub paint into metal Alphabet Charms and photo corner and wipe of excess.

2. Stamp flower image onto canvas with acrylic paint. Paint edges of Defined sticker and place on top.

3. Paint scrap of watercolor paper, adhere and tie ribbon across. Edge travel tag with same color paint and attach with snaps.

4. Lightly wipe paint over textured paper pieces to emphasize pattern. Layer with other painted pieces.

5. Rub paint in Charmed Phrase and wipe away excess. Stamp image onto back of transparency sheet with paint and attach.

6. Paint inside and around edges of Charmed Plaque.

7

brush techniques

Don't think of it as a paintbrush. Think of it as a magic wand. You'll be astounded at the array of effects you can create with a few simple swipes of paint. Try dry brushing to add depth and dimension to distressed embellishments or to create the casual look of denim. Just make sure you try it—you're sure to get enchanting results.

DRY BRUSHING PATTERNS

1. Punch or cut out shapes or strips and arrange as desired.

2. Dry brush vertically and horizontally with paint in crosshatch pattern.

1. Apply a small amount of paint to palette, lightly dip in stipple brush and pounce on paper towel. On light blue cardstock, dry brush vertically with medium blue paint.

2. Dry brush horizontally with dark blue paint.

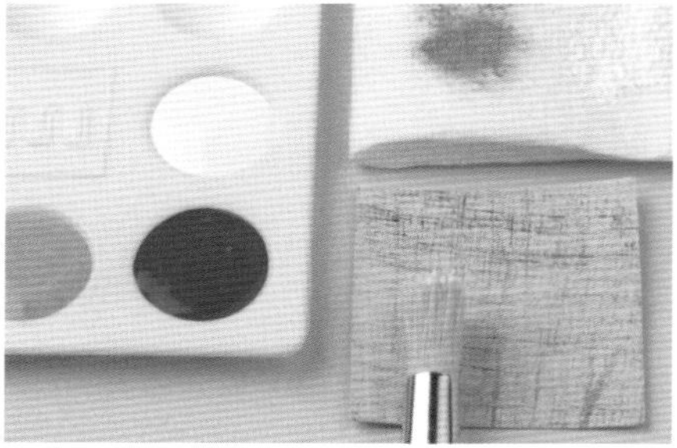

3. Lightly go over piece with white paint.

SHARE *by Rhonda Solomon*

Alphabet rub-ons, ribbon, scrapbook colors acrylic paint: Making Memories; Stamps: All Night Media and Postmodern Design; Other: Bracelet toggle

how to: Create background paper using drybrush technique. Punch out small square photos, mat and adhere. Mat and attach main photo. Create title on punched and cut scraps of cardstock with a combination of stamped and embossed letters and rub-ons. Add printed words in white on black. Add toggle and ribbon along side.

1 2 3

4 5 6

VARIATIONS *by Rhonda Solomon*

1. Dry brush snowflake Eyelet Charm with pale pink paint and attach to frame with ribbons.

2. Punch ID tag shape out of black and white photo. Dry brush edges with blue paint and coat with Diamond Glaze.

3. Create stamped and embellished mini envelope. Melt wax over flap and impress initials to seal. When cool, dry brush with white paint.

4. Dry brush woven strips of light and dark blue cardstock with black paint and stitch to denim.

5. Paint Charmed Frame pink, dry brush with black paint and sand. Dry brush Blossom with white paint and attach to cardstock square with brad.

6. Paint letter stencil. Stamp words and emboss using white powder. Dry brush with white paint.

8

stencils

There are a few things that just go together. Peanut butter and jelly, Bogey and Bacall, stencils and acrylic paint. But there's so much more than simply setting down a stencil and dabbing paint inside. Apply various layers through a letter or shape to create depth and texture, or sand and paint the stencils themselves to create a title or accent. Be brave with your stencils and you'll get both beauty and style.

k
S

STENCIL IDEAS

1. Once stencil image is painted, add words, stripes or patterns before you remove the stencil.

1. Stamp word using foam stamps and black ink.

2. Cut around stamped images with a craft knife, making sure to set aside any inside parts of the letters. Cut stenciled letters out in rectangular shapes and place on background.

3. Dab paint in stencils and around outside edges. Remove and cut out around stamped images to create letter blocks. Use stencils over and over again or use actual stencil on other projects.

4. Try using this technique with any font or word printed from your computer.

ERIN—JOURNEY *by Erin Terrell*

Computer font: Incognitype TrueType; Embossing powder: Ranger Industries; Foam stamps, magnetic date stamp and scrapbook colors acrylic paint: Making Memories; Stamping inks: Colorbox and Versamark; Stamps: Magenta; Stickers: K&Company; Other: Chipboard and walnut ink

how to: Crumple background piece of cream cardstock, dip in walnut ink, flatten and let dry. Leave overnight under stack of books or other weight to flatten completely. Cut a wide strip of cream cardstock and stamp with Versamark ink and clock stamp. Coat with embossing powder and heat. Crumple strip, dip in walnut ink, flatten, let dry and attach across bottom. Add strips of blue paper to either side of strip and mat photo on same blue paper. Edge photo with paint. Print journaling, edge with paint and add label stickers. Stamp title on chipboard using Custom Stencils technique. Stamp date and place below title.

1

4

2

5

3

6
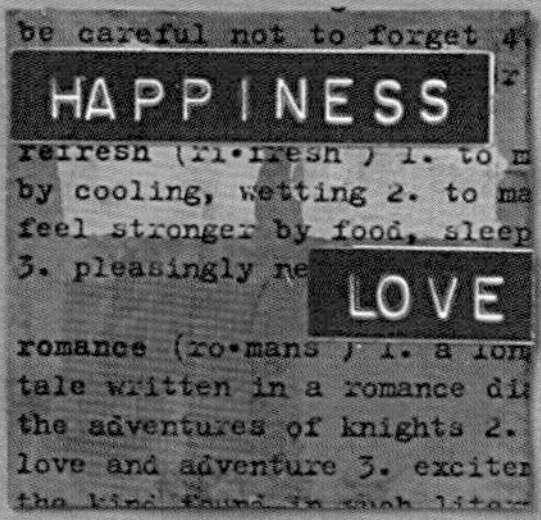

VARIATIONS *by Erin Terrell*

1. Mix paint with Liquitex Paint Thickener and dab through stencil to create a raised surface.

2. Stencil numbers on cardstock and stamp script image on top with paint.

3. Hold flower stencil to page, ink through with Versamark pad and heat emboss with clear powder. Dab paint over image with foam brush.

4. Cut out letters from stencil templates, sand and coat with paint to create monogram embellishments or to spell words.

5. Stencil flower on paper. Let dry, position stencil in same place as before and stamp through with text stamp and paint.

6. Use basket weave stencil and various colors of paint to create a color blocked background.

9

embellishments

Leave the house without earrings and a handbag and you might feel incomplete. Believe it or not, your layouts can feel the same way. Embellishments are the accessories that pull your pages together. Add a fresh coat of paint to surfaces, grooves and edges to make them unique and individual. Just like a great pair of designer stilettos.

elebrate

PAINTING AND HEAT EMBOSSING

1. Sand metal piece with sanding block and coat with paint. Add second coat if desired.

2. When dry, press metal piece into Versamark ink. Coat with Ultrathick Embossing Enamel and heat set.

3. Repeat step 2 to create a smooth, bubble-like finish.

1. Lightly sand metal using fine grit sandpaper or sanding block.

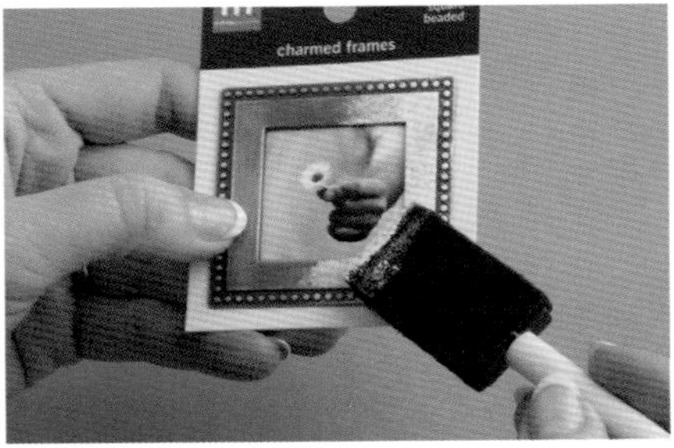

2. Apply coat of paint with a foam brush, holding brush flat to piece. Use little pressure to avoid getting paint into grooves.

3. Add second coat of paint if desired.

POINT CABRILLO *by Erin Terrell*

Alphabet charms, alphabet rub-ons, charmed frame, charmed photo corner, defined, scrapbook colors acrylic paint and word fetti: Making Memories; Foil: Staedler; Paper: Making Memories

how to: Create layered background with three colors of cardstock. Add Defined stickers along each side and rub foil in the top right hand corner, covering part of the sticker. Mat photo, adhere and place strip of cardstock in bottom corner, overlapping part of the photo. Add Word Fetti stickers randomly around page. Paint frame, letters and photo corner and attach to layout, inserting accent photo under frame. Finish title with alphabet rub-ons.

1 2 3

4 5 6

VARIATIONS *by Erin Terrell*

1. Paint entire surface of Metal Word in a single color.

2. Rub paint into grooves of Alphabet Charms and letters stamped with Metal Stamps and wipe away excess.

3. Sand and paint metal flower. Paint back of Page Pebble with contrasting color and attach as center.

4. Rub paint into letters on Charmed Words and Charmed Phrases and wipe away excess.

5. Dab paint on metal-rimmed tag with foam brush.

6. Heat emboss painted embellishments for a shiny finish.

10
texture into paint

Ginseng, gingko and guarana. Go to any smoothie shop and you'll find an endless menu of add-ins that transform frozen fruit into an energy elixir. Boost your paint by adding in a thickening agent or two. You'll get a different finish and texture with each one—shiny, matte, sandy and more. Swipe thickened paint across a page, dab it through stencils or run a little along the edges for a refreshing change to your pages.

THICKENER

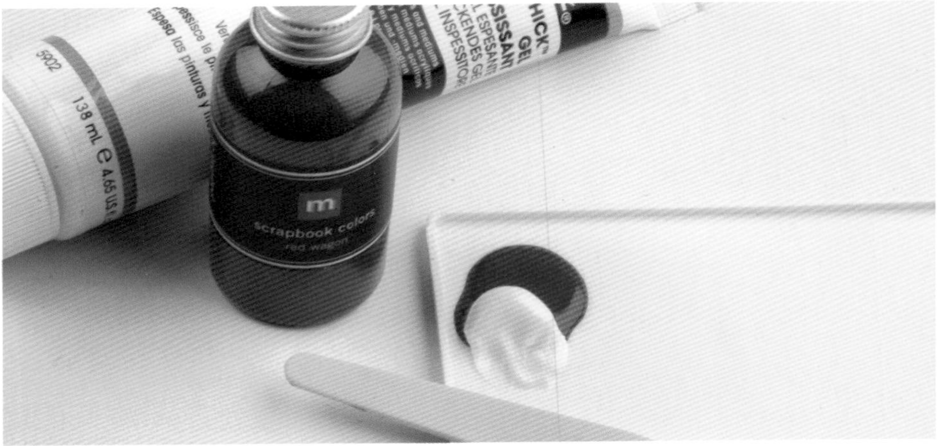

1. Mix paint with a very small amount of Liquithick thickener until desired texture is achieved. Add more paint if consistency is too dry or add more thickener if consistency is too wet.

2. Paint background paper with various colors of regular acrylic paint. Use a foam brush to dab on thickened paint in lines as design dictates.

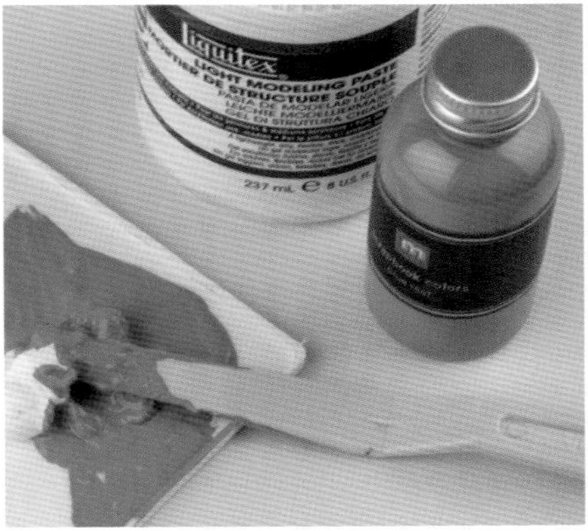

1. Mix modeling paste with desired paint color.

2. Tape stencil to painted background and smear paint mixture over stencil with palette knife. Scrape off excess.

2. Remove stencil and wash quickly to remove paste.

If you don't like something change it. If you can't change it, change your attitude. ~Maya Angelou
ATTITUDE
Erin Terrell
April 2004
Do not go where the path may lead, go instead where there is no path & leave a trail. ~Ralph Waldo Emerson

ATTITUDE *by Erin Terrell*

Computer font: Incognitype TrueType; Lettering template: Scrap Pagerz; Paint thickener: Liquitex Liquithick; Scrapbook colors acrylic paint: Making Memories; Stamping ink: Ranger Industries

how to: Create background using Thickener technique. Mat and adhere photo and print quotes on white cardstock. Edge with black ink and attach to layout. Dab thickened paint through lettering template to create title down right side.

1

2

3

4
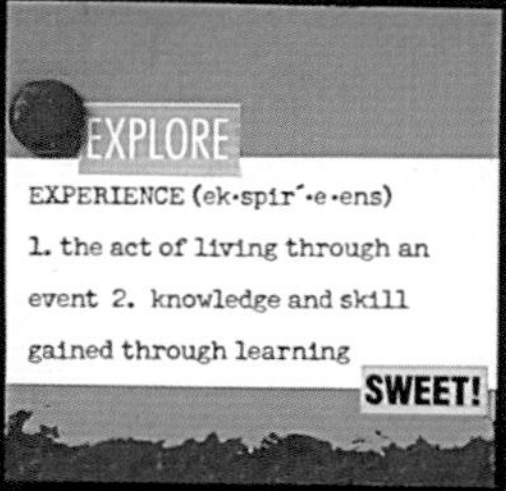

5

6

VARIATIONS *by Erin Terrell*

1. Add Liquitex Resin Sand Texture to paint, mix and fill in surface of Metal Mesh.

2. Mix Liquitex Black Lava Texture Gel with paint and brush a thick stripe across middle of page. Result will be a shiny finish.

3. Use foam brush to dab thickened paint through stencil letters. Edge Defined stickers with thickened paint.

4. Dab thickened paint along edge of background to create a raised, textured border.

5. Mix Liquitex Glass Beads Texture Gel with paint, fill in middle of frame and press in an embellishment.

6. Add Light Modeling Paste to paint and cover background. Coat metal embellishments with Liquithick Gel Thickener mixed with paint.

"I have so much fun adding texture to paints to see what I can come up with. I feel like a kid again mixing up concoctions to see what kind of interesting results I can get. It's all in good fun."

ERIN TERRELL

IDEA GALLERY

BIRTHDAY *by Rhonda Solomon*

Alphabet charms, artisan labels, eyelet letters, eyelets, magnetic date stamp, ribbon, scrapbook colors acrylic paint and stitches: Making Memories; Doilies: Artifacts, Inc.; Other: Leaf charm and straight pins

how to: Dry brush textured cardstock with blue paint to create background paper. Paint doilies with coordinating colors and attach. Rub various colors of paint into letters, wipe off excess, dry brush over top and place along top. Paint numbers, attach through photo with eyelets and tie with Stitches. Print journaling and stamp date on artisan labels and attach. Add leaf charm to edge, tie ribbon in upper corner and secure ends with pins.

CARTER *by Rhonda Solomon*

Adhesive: Decoupage Matte by Plaid; Alphabet stamps, defined clear, magnetic date stamp, mini tags, ribbon, ribbon charms and scrapbook colors acrylic paint: Making Memories; Decorative scissors: Fiskars; Paper: Bazzill; Stencil: Plaid; Other: Beads, sandpaper and thread

how to: With dry stencil brush, stipple acrylic paint over stencil to create background. Brush paint along edges of cardstock. When paint is dry, crinkle and open paper several times and sand. Paint Ribbon Charms, sand edges, brush on decoupage medium and tie with ribbons. Add printed journaling and Defined to cardstock, adding Mini Tags and beads. Mat photo, trim with decorative scissors and stitch to page with zigzag stitch.

REFLECTIONS AT 30 *by Emily Waters*

Artisan labels, brad, eyelets, foam stamps, magnetic alphabet stamps, ribbon, scrapbook colors acrylic paint and staples: Making Memories; Paper: Making Memories; Other: Acetate and ribbon

how to: Cover two-thirds of background paper with vertical and horizontal strokes of paint. Stamp word along remaining area of page with foam stamps. Stamp numbers on cardstock, trim and attach with staples. Print title on acetate and attach using eyelets and ribbon. Fold and stitch acetate to create a pocket and edge with paint. Add journaling in Ledger Paper envelope embellished with Artisan Label and ribbon tab top. Tuck into pocket.

SIMPLE *by Emily Waters*

Alphabet stamps: PSX Design; Charmed frame, eyelets, paper, ribbon, rub-ons and scrapbook colors acrylic paint: Making Memories; Fabric: Rachel Ashwell; Other: Acetate

how to: Attach fabric to chipboard and, with a sewing machine, stitch around edges to secure. Trim papers for matting and edge all layers with acrylic paint. Attach photo to mat and place acetate over the top. Apply rub-ons randomly to cover acetate. Turn acetate over and mask off area to highlight. Paint in desired area and remove tape. Edge outside of Charmed Frame with paint, place on square of fabric and stamp title with paint. Finish by attaching acetate to rest of layout with ribbon tied between two eyelets.

March 27th 2004
CASEY
11
CASEY
11
the
Determination
of a child

THE DETERMINATION OF A CHILD *by Emily Waters*

Alphabet rub-ons, foam stamps, label holder, magnetic date stamp, ribbon and scrapbook colors acrylic paint: Making Memories; Other: Chipboard

how to: Paint first color on alphabet foam stamps and stamp title across bottom of background. Once dry, stamp same letters on top using a different color, slightly offsetting placement to create a shadow effect. Sand edges of photos and arrange on layout. Complete title using alphabet rub-ons. Add Label Holder and attach with strips of ribbon. Edge perimeter of background with paint.

Casey lost 2 of his bottom middle teeth in the same week. He was so excited and couldn't wait for the tooth fairy to visit him. He decided that he wanted to take the teeth to show and tell and waited to put them under his pillow until he could show off his new lost teeth at school. He is such a joy to be around and we cherish each moment we have with him.
A MOMENT IN Time
Date: 5 03

A MOMENT IN TIME *by Emily Waters*

Alphabet stamps, foam stamps, ledger paper, scrapbook colors acrylic paint and screw snap: Making Memories; Paper: Chatterbox and Making Memories; Stamps: Missing Link Stamp Company; Other: Acetate, fabric, old dictionary paper and stencil

how to: Paint stencil alphabet desired color and back with dictionary paper. Cut a piece of fabric the length of the page. Stamp title along fabric with acrylic paint. Print journaling on acetate and highlight desired words by painting on back. Cut out date from ledger paper and adhere to bottom of stencil alphabet. Attach group to layout and mount and tuck photo under fabric strip.

enjoy
[suc·cess]
The highest reward for a persons work is not what they get for it, but what they become by it.
Heidi, Bridgette, Robin, and Emily
Taping of Martha Stewart
Heber, Utah
February 9, 2004

ENJOY SUCCESS *by Emily Waters*

Eyelet charms, magnetic alphabet stamps, metal frames, ribbon, rub-ons, scrapbook colors acrylic paint and snaps: Making Memories; Paper: Chatterbox; Other: Acetate

how to: Print quote on acetate and create pocket by stitching around bottom and two sides. Mat photo on patterned paper, fold sides over and stitch down to attach. Cut corner off Metal Frame and slightly sand corner and Eyelet Charm tags. Paint all metal surfaces with pink paint and let dry. Wrap ribbon around center of page and attach Eyelet Charm tag. Punch hole in both sides of Metal Frame corner and tie back together with a piece of ribbon. Fold Eyelet Charm tags around bottom edge of layout and attach acetate journaling with snaps.

LITTLE LIZZIE *by Robin Johnson*

Blossoms, decorative brads, rub-ons, scrapbook colors acrylic paint, vellum tag: Making Memories; Corner stencil: Plaid; Fabric: Rachel Ashwell; Tag: DMD; Other: Letter stencil

how to: Tear fabric and adhere to background with spray adhesive. Tear strips of coordinating fabric, punch holes in top and bottom corners of left side and tie strips through. Place photo and stencil at opposite corners. Stencil letter on tag and wait for it to dry. Place stencil over letter again, hold in place and apply rub-ons on top of the painted letter. Rub paint into two Decorative Brads, lightly sand and use as centers to attach Blossoms. Apply rub-on to vellum tag and wrap around outside edge.

SEASHORE MEMORIES *by Robin Johnson*

Artisan labels, defined mini, eyelets, jump rings, magnetic alphabet stamps and scrapbook colors acrylic paint: Making Memories; Beads: Cousin Corp.; Embroidery floss: DMC; Stamping ink: Tsukineko; Watercolor paper: Strathmore; Other: Waxed linen

how to: Use Wash technique to paint background color. Let page dry. Tear off 1/2 inch from each end and adhere left strip on right edge and right strip on left edge. Glue center piece down. Mat photo with extra watercolor paper. Wash over Artisan Labels with complementary colors and cut up to create photo corner and tag. Wash over Defined Mini sticker and add to page with eyelets. Tie floss through to secure. Attach small tag with jump rings, add beaded waxed linen and stamp title.

CUDDLE BUG *by Rhonda Solomon*

Brad, eyelet letters, foam stamps, hinges, label holder, safety pins, scrapbook colors acrylic paint and washer words: Making Memories; Glitter: Magic Scraps; Paper: Making Memories; Other: Ribbon

how to: Trace bugs on white cardstock for accents and decorate with paint and glitter. Mat on blocks of printed paper and attach to background. Paint Eyelet Letters and Label Holder with matching paint, adhere and stamp remaining title with foam stamps. Dry brush horizontally and vertically over background and accents with black paint. Attach photo to layout with Hinges, adding journaling underneath. Slide Washer Word onto ribbon and tie through eyelet and one side of Label Holder.

FALL MEMORIES *by Robin Johnson*

Leather corner, leather frame and scrapbook colors acrylic paint: Making Memories; Modeling paste: Artquest; Stencil: Plaid; Tags: Nostalgiques, EK Success; Twine: Hillcreek Designs

how to: Mix paint with modeling paste, dab onto edges of cardstock and smear randomly with a palette knife to create textured background. Add wide, vertical strip of paper and adhere main photo on top. Mix second color of paint into modeling paste for leaf accent. Using a palette knife, smear mixture across a stencil, remove carefully and let pattern dry. Tear around edges, tie tags to design with twine and hand letter remaining title. Wet Leather Frame and stamp letters with metal alphabet stamps. Place accent photo underneath and attach. Add Leather Corner to photo and adhere journaling strips with various knots and stitches.

determination
POCAHONTAS
Daisy decided to dress as Pocahontas for Halloween this year, so MiMi graciously agreed to sew her costume once again. When it arrived in the mail, Daisy was so excited that she immediately had to put it on. We had a hard time making her wait until Halloween to actually wear it out of the house!
personality
strength
spirit

POCAHONTAS *by Erin Terrell*

Alphabet stamps: Hero Arts; Charmed photo corner, foam stamps, ribbon and scrapbook colors acrylic paint: Making Memories; Computer font: Incognitype; Stickers: K&Company

how to: Paint strips of cardstock green and let dry. Edge borders of background paper with paint and foam brush and dab a second color around corners. Adhere green border strips to page and line edges with ribbon. Place photos and add label stickers to each. Stamp edges with decorative foam stamp, overlapping some of the photos. Print journaling, edge with paint and attach. Finish by stamping title and adding photo corner.

"Paint is my new favorite scrapbooking supply. What can't you do with it? Seriously."

EMILY WATERS

"I love mixing colors, blending colors and creating colors that match my photos perfectly."

ROBIN JOHNSON

ARTISTS AUTHOR

1. ROBIN JOHNSON
Farmington, Utah
FIVE THINGS THAT HELP ME RELAX WHEN I'M STRESSED:
· Eating a Krispy Kreme doughnut.
· Playing the piano really loud.
· Calling a sister or friend.
· Jumping on the trampoline with my kids.
· Taking a yoga class.

2. RHONDA SOLOMON
Snowflake, Arizona
FOUR TRUTHS AND A LIE ABOUT RHONDA SOLOMON:
· Favorite background scrapbooking movies: Anne of Green Gables and Anne of Avonlea.
· Favorite reading material: Cookbooks.
· Favorite breakfast: Diet Coke (even better when accompanied by a chocolate chip cookie).
· Favorite season: Fall.
· Favorite hobby: NASCAR Racing.

3. ERIN TERRELL
San Antonio, Texas
FIVE THINGS I BET YOU DIDN'T KNOW ABOUT ME:
· I am an expert at making grilled cheese sandwiches.
· I blast Linkin Park on my iPod while I'm scrapping.
· I Photoshop the heck out of my pictures.
· I never drive the speed limit.
· I always wear multiple toe rings.

4. EMILY WATERS
Draper, Utah
WILL THE REAL EMILY WATERS PLEASE STAND UP?
· I enjoy the surprise of arriving home to see what fabulous thing my decorator Beth has done.
· When it's my turn to choose a restaurant, it's Mexican food.
· I own 5 pairs of pink shoes, 21 pairs of red shoes and 32 pairs of capris. It's sick, I know.
· What my TV is tuned to constantly—HGTV.
· If you know any tall, dark, handsome, single men, please give them my number.

5. JENNIFER KOFFORD *writer*
Ogden, Utah
A FEW OF MY DAYDREAMS:
· Traveling to all seven continents in the world (tally so far is four).
· Living in New York City.
· Appearing in a major motion picture.
· Spending an entire week scrapbooking surrounded by good friends and good food (and no interruptions!).
· Driving a Honda Pilot with a DVD player.